Original title:
Trailing Ivy Dreams

Copyright © 2025 Creative Arts Management OÜ
All rights reserved.

Author: Colin Leclair
ISBN HARDBACK: 978-1-80581-843-4
ISBN PAPERBACK: 978-1-80581-370-5
ISBN EBOOK: 978-1-80581-843-4

The Poetry of Climbing Silence

In a garden where whispers hide,
Cucumbers dance, they glide and slide.
The daisies gossip, all in a row,
While broccoli claims to be the star of the show.

A snail on a mission, slow as can be,
Wonders aloud, "Is this the real me?"
The grasshoppers laugh, with a leap and a cheer,
As tomatoes blush, all red with no fear.

Harbored Secrets in Leafy Corners

Underneath the ferns, secrets abound,
A rabbit's last carrot he thinks he has found.
The worms throw a party, their music divine,
While the turnips roll in—a veggie confine.

The raccoon spins tales of late night affairs,
In the shadows he schemed with the garden's own pears.
A stolen cupcake, in orange and teal,
The laughter of nature is all too surreal.

The Arc of Imagination's Vines

The beans climb high, with dreams in their eyes,
Telling tall tales under cotton-ball skies.
Zucchini invents new dance moves each day,
While the sunflowers cheer, come what may.

An echo of giggles from petals that sway,
With bees in tuxedos, they come out to play.
Imaginations sprout with each sprig of thyme,
In this garden of laughter, growing sublime.

Dreams Woven in the Foliage

In shadows of green, dreams start to weave,
Carrots in capes on a mission to leave.
Potatoes inventing grand stories of flight,
While the onions all giggle, eyes sparkling bright.

With ivy as tales, they twirl and they wind,
A winged cucumber, unique and unkind.
Through the leaves, imagination shines bright,
In a funny old garden, everything's right.

Cairn of Hidden Longings

In the garden of wishes, I planted a stone,
Hoping to grow a tall tale of my own.
But squirrels seem keen on my dreams of a plant,
They've formed a baking club—oh, how they chant!

Each pebble a thought, a quirky delight,
The daisies are giggling, it's quite a sight.
With marshmallow clouds and a pancake sun,
I swore I'd outsmart them, but now I'm just done.

The shadows are winking, the gnomes have a say,
They're plotting a party, hip-hip-hooray!
My longing's a Cairn, a hapless old joke,
And I'm just the fool, who can't find the cloak.

Serpentine Hues of Serenity

A lizard in shades of a banana peel,
Slithers on by with a comical feel.
It twirls in the sunlight, so sly and so spry,
While dragonflies giggle and ask him to fly.

With colors so wacky, it crafts a design,
A pattern so goofy, it rivals the vine.
The sky gives a chuckle, the grass starts to sway,
As all of nature laughs in a whimsical way.

Oh, the hues of a serpent's most serene escapades,
Turn dull lizards into a circus parade.
A dance of delight in the big leafy trees,
I'd trade all my worries for moments like these.

In the Arms of the Wild

I wandered the woods, quite lost and confused,
Where branches would tattle, and bushes just snooze.
A bear offered tea and a chocolate cake,
Said, 'Join me for laughter, for goodness' sake!'

The owls threw a rave with a disco ball shine,
While rabbits in bowties danced in a line.
With nature's own band on a merrymaking spree,
I laughed so hard, I snorted my tea.

In the wild's loving arms, I twirled and I spun,
Where every odd moment was joyfully fun.
An iguana in heels led the conga parade,
As I felt all my troubles instantly fade.

Unfurling Stories on the Trellis

My stories are creeping like vines on a wall,
Chasing after sunlight, answering the call.
With tales of mishaps and gaffes I have made,
Each leaf tells a rumor that's widely portrayed.

A beetle in glasses surveys the whole scene,
While ladybugs plot with their mischievous gleam.
And as night approaches, they gather around,
Spinning yarns of the silly, where laughter is found.

Each tendril causing chuckles, a whimsical spree,
"Did you hear what he said? You won't believe me!"
Unfurling connections like a wobbly dance,
In this garden of stories, they all take a chance.

Secrets in the Green Canopy

Beneath the leaves, a gnome spins,
He juggles acorns, grinning wins.
The squirrels giggle, tails in flight,
As fairies dance in pure delight.

A hedgehog wears a tiny hat,
While rabbits play a game with that.
The mushrooms cheer, a raucous crowd,
As nature laughs, both bright and loud.

Echoes of Nature's Embrace

A toad sings opera from a pond,
While crickets cheer, a raucous bond.
The flowers sway, they hum along,
In this sweet place, all feel strong.

Bumblebees form a buzzing band,
Playing tunes across the land.
With chatter loud, the trees conspire,
To spread the joy, lift spirits higher.

Lush Reveries at Dusk

The sun dips low, a golden blush,
As fireflies flicker in a rush.
A raccoon struts, wearing bling,
With twinkling eyes, he starts to sing.

A curious owl joins the fray,
Dropping jokes, come what may.
The whispers in the leaves declare,
In this wild dance, nothing's rare.

Tangles of Time and Memory

Old vines twist in a playful tease,
Their stories mix with rustling leaves.
A forgotten shoe dangles high,
While lizards laugh as they stroll by.

Pine cones roll like tiny balls,
Among the roots, the laughter calls.
As shadows stretch and colors blend,
Nature's humor knows no end.

Mementos of a Serpent's Path

In the garden, snakes do twist,
They weave through flowers, can't resist.
With a flick of tail, they clearly say,
"Watch your step, don't tread my way!"

But when they laugh, it's quite a sight,
Slithering softly, day or night.
They guard the secrets, bold and bright,
In a wiggly dance, they take flight.

Hues of an Enchanted Climb

Up the wall, colors fight and roam,
A vine decides to call it home.
With a little twist and a vibrant shout,
It claims the space, there's no doubt.

Painted petals watch it tease,
A wobbly dance on a gentle breeze.
Leaves giggle softly, tickled by air,
"We'll grow together—don't you dare!"

The Soft Undercurrent of Green

Amidst the grass, a party's set,
Where bugs do tango and frogs all bet.
The daisies cheer with laughter high,
As twirling ants just drift on by.

Mossy beats thump between the roots,
A dance-off starts with funny hoots.
Laughter erupts from all around,
In squishy shoes on slippery ground.

Dreams Unfurled in the Bower

In a nook where shadows play,
A squirrel dreams the day away.
With acorns piled and leaves like beds,
He dreams of stardust on his heads.

A breeze comes in, it tickles ears,
And whispers tales that bring forth cheers.
"Join the fun!" the old tree beams,
As all of nature joins in dreams!

Whispers of the Climbing Green

A leaf once told a joke to me,
It giggled as it swayed so free.
'Why did the vine embrace the wall?
To catch a break at the gardener's call!'

In shadows where the laughter weaves,
Creeping greens play games with leaves.
'Take my hand!' they tease and twine,
While squirrels dance along the vine!

Secrets in the Twisted Vines

Underneath the tangled mess,
Rabbits plan their sneaky press.
'Why not steal that carrot bright?
It's hiding well, like a ninja at night!'

The vines conspire with a chuckle,
As birds plot schemes and can't help but chuckle.
'Who will riddle the gardener's mind?
Watch us unravel the trails we find!'

Echoes of the Verdant Heart

A fern once sang a silly tune,
As ants marched under the glowing moon.
'Frogs croak louder than my beat,
But I've got style, and my leaves are sweet!'

Dandelions laughed at the hare,
'Take it slow, don't go anywhere!
Chase your dreams, but hop with flair,
Or find yourself lost in a fanciful snare!'

A Tapestry of Leaves

Woven threads of green delight,
Frogs debate, 'Can we take flight?'
A butterfly laughs, 'Just flap a bit,
But don't forget to show some wit!'

The sun pokes fun at the wilting blooms,
'Come dance with me in your leafy rooms!'
Amidst the laughter and gentle tease,
Nature hides secrets with playful ease.

The Caress of Lush Shadows

In a garden of giggles, I hide away,
Where plants wear faces, and squirrels display.
A vine whispers secrets, dressed up in green,
Tickling my ankles, it's quite the routine.

A mushroom's a hat for a gopher parade,
While daisies gossip in sunshine parades.
The petals wear slippers, their dance is divine,
As frogs in tuxedos hold court over wine.

Bumblebees buzz with a riotous cheer,
They sip on the nectar and fill up with beer.
The day's antics weave through the soft, leafy veil,
While bushes break into a light-hearted tale.

In this playground of leaves, I chuckle and grin,
For nature's a jester, inviting me in.
With laughter and whimsy, I sway like a leaf,
In shadows that cradle my heart with belief.

Vines of Memory's Song

With each twist and twirl, the vines weave a tune,
Reminding me of laughter beneath the bright moon.
A hedgehog once juggled, oh what a delight,
While crickets provided a musical night.

The flowers are chatting, their tales rather bold,
Of bees on a quest for the finest of gold.
The wisteria winks, should I dance on a stage?
While butterflies giggle, suggesting it's age.

A vine wraps around me, it feels like a hug,
As a snail passes by with a charismatic shrug.
We share little secrets, the vine and I play,
In a battle of wits, who'll win the day?

Nature's a circus; there's fun everywhere,
The laughter of petals floats sweetly on air.
And I join the frolic, by whimsy beguiled,
In a world where the green is forever wild.

Echoes of Climbing Whispers

In a forest of laughter, the ivy will climb,
Telling tales of mischief, one giggle at a time.
A raccoon in pajamas sneaks late night snacks,
While owls roll their eyes at his quirky antics.

The roots are like gossip, they weave and they snare,
Planting tiny chuckles in rich, fertile air.
A cricket atop a mushroom takes flight,
Launching a joke that takes off in delight.

The sun peeks through branches, like a joyful muse,
While ferns flex their fronds in their vibrant green hues.
Marigolds burst forth with a witty remark,
As shadows dance softly, igniting a spark.

Every rustle and whisper, a riddle, a jest,
Nature's own comedy, delivering the best.
I'll parade with the leaves, in this whimsical gang,
While climbing the laughter, as nature's bells rang.

Dreamlike Patterns in the Underbrush

In the underbrush maze where the trails intertwine,
The squirrels do cartwheels, like stars in decline.
The daisies draw maps with their petals so bright,
While fireflies giggle, lighting up the night.

Spiders weave stories on silken fine thread,
While mushrooms play chess with a soft, tangled head.
A butterfly flutters, won't you join my team?
As we dance on the breeze in a whimsical dream.

A hedgehog wears glasses, reaching for crumbs,
While a mouse bends to listen to nature's old drums.
The beat of the laughter, it echoes so sweet,
As I trip over roots, in my hurry to greet.

With each playful jest, the forest comes alive,
In patterns of fun, where the silly can thrive.
And I lose myself, oh what joyous conundrum,
In a world of pure chuckles, where I feel so welcome.

Chasing Echoes of the Rustling Green

In the garden where giggles grow,
Worms wear ties, and daisies flow.
A squirrel with shades, doing the twist,
Balloons on the branches, they can't be missed.

Grasshoppers dance in shoes too tight,
As beetles play cards late at night.
The daisies debate the best comic book,
While the trees share secrets with a knowing nook.

Fragments of a Leafy Story

Once a leaf told tales quite absurd,
Of a hedgehog who thought he could fly like a bird.
He donned a cape made of moss and glee,
But the branches just chuckled, 'Oh, let it be!'

Next to a brook where whispers giggle,
A frog tried ballet, oh how he did wiggle!
His tutu was lily pads, quite the sight,
As fish cheered him on with all of their might.

The Sweet Surrender of Nature's Touch

The roses gossip of shady affairs,
While the sun throws confetti in golden layers.
A snail with a top hat, oh, what a swell,
Regales the daisies with tales of his shell.

A bee in a beanie buzzes about,
Proclaiming his dream to sing and to shout.
While branches join in, swaying with grace,
A laughter erupts in the green, wild space.

Tapestry of Cloven Shadows

On a cloudy day, shadows debate,
Whether to dance or meditate.
The breeze brings chuckles, soft and light,
As squirrels set up a theater at night.

An owl with glasses, reading the news,
Announces the latest in silly shoes.
While the plants chime in, making a fuss,
About grass stains on the bus.

Through the Green-Laced Arches

A squirrel in a tux, what a sight,
Dancing with the leaves, in moonlight.
He twirls with grace, a real charmer,
Such style, you'd think, he's got a farmer.

A rabbit wearing shades hops by,
Shouting, "Hey, buddy, let's catch that pie!"
While birds in suits gossip and caw,
Making fashion statements, breaking the law!

Flowers gossip, trading faux pas,
"Your blooms are bold, but your scent's a flaw!"
Yet under arches, they all unite,
In laughter and whimsy, such pure delight.

So wander through gardens, don't be shy,
Join the frog choir, give a loud sigh!
In this green lace, mirth takes the stage,
Where every step's a new, silly page.

Underneath the Secreted Sky

Beneath the sky, a cat wears a crown,
Declaring he's king of this quirky town.
He rules with whimsy, on a whim, of course,
While mice in tuxedos plot a quick course.

A hedgehog juggles acorns with flair,
Claiming he's training for the county fair.
He spins and he twirls, quite the display,
But every few moments, he rolls away!

Fluffy clouds giggle as they drift by,
With unicorns prancing, oh my, oh my!
They whisper sweet secrets only they share,
Underneath the skies, we lose all despair.

So drop your worries, join us today,
In this silly realm where we laugh and play.
With every chuckle, your heart will start,
To dance with joy and awaken your heart.

Tendrils of Forgotten Wishes

In the garden of dreams, gnomes like to chat,
Dreaming of spaces where wishes grow fat.
One says, "I wish for a garden so wide,
With pizza trees growing, right by my side!"

With flowers that giggle, petals that tease,
Every whimsy blooms with the greatest of ease.
A snail in a hat, gossiping tall tales,
Shares stories of knights wearing pink polka scales.

Marigolds chuckle, with faces so bright,
"Do you think frogs care if they hop left or right?"
Yet all the while, they bounce and they play,
Wishing on petals that drift far away.

So let's weave our wishes on vines hanging low,
And laugh with the blooms as they start to glow.
In this garden of nonsense, come spin your delight,
Where even the mundane feels fanciful and bright.

The Climb Towards the Unseen

A squirrel climbed high, on branches he clings,
Dreaming of acorns and other fine things.
He plots and he schemes as he starts to ascend,
Wishing for treasures that never will end.

Up goes the hamster, his heart full of cheer,
In a tiny red car, he's shifting to gear.
"Faster!" he squeaks, with his tiny paws strained,
While the hedgehog just watches, a bit entertained.

The branches all sway, creating a stage,
Where laughter and antics take center page.
With a twist and a turn, they soar through the air,
Chasing the flutters of pixies' sweet hair.

So climb towards the unknown, my merry friends,
And giggle at nature's delightful bends.
For in the great heights, we'll craft our own tale,
Where the silly and sweet intertwine without fail.

Enchanted by the Climbing Shade

In the garden, green vines twirl,
They tickle my toes as I give a whirl.
What are they plotting, those leafy crews?
I swear they giggle, sharing their views.

Beneath the arch of nature's spree,
The shadows play tricks, oh woe is me!
A leaf took my hat, then dashed away,
I will get it back, just wait for the day!

Chasing shadows 'round every bend,
These sneaky vines, my playful friends.
They tug at my sleeves, beg for a feast,
Are they here for fun, or just a tease?

Among the emerald, laughter swells,
In the green maze, I weave my spells.
With vines on my shoulders, I take my stand,
Who knew my garden had a comedy band?

Veils of Verdant Hopes

Under the cloak of leafy dreams,
Plants whisper secrets in soft moonbeams.
Corners where shadows and giggles blend,
Creating mischief, they twist and bend.

A vine wiggles like it's got a plan,
I thought it was a bush, but now it ran!
If plants could chat, what tales they'd weave,
Of past adventures that make you believe.

The dandelions chuckle, all in a bunch,
As I tell my woes over a garden lunch.
They grow in a patch, like they own the cart,
Little do they know, I've got a big heart.

So here's to the green, where laughter rolls,
A world full of wonders tickling our souls.
I'll dance with the vines, let silliness bloom,
In this leafy jungle, there's always more room!

Nostalgic Hues Among the Leaves

In hues of green where memories sprout,
A slip of a vine gives a joyful shout.
I trip over roots, stumble and sway,
They seem to laugh, come join the play!

The daisies smile, in pastel attire,
While dandelion wishes catch summer's fire.
With laughter aloft, they spin and twirl,
Suddenly my troubles begin to unfurl.

The breeze carries jokes from flower to tree,
Revealing the humor in nature's spree.
Every petal a giggle, every leaf a laugh,
In this nostalgic garden, I'd take a photograph.

Oh, the memories of days filled with glee,
As I wander through greens, nature sets me free.
With each vine that curls and bends just right,
I find joy in shadows, and laughter in light.

The Dance of Nature's Fingers

The trees sway gently, choreographed play,
With nature's fingers guiding the way.
A breeze, a twirl, oh what a sight,
Leaves doing ballet in the soft twilight.

An acorn dropped, causing a mess,
Watch out, dear squirrel, you've made a distress!
With flourishes wild, they tumble and preen,
I laugh at the antics that make life serene.

The ferns do the tango, oh what a scene,
While petals pirouette, like dancers so keen.
Nature is giggling with every laugh,
As vines shimmy by, not caring for a path.

So come join the frolic, let's give it a whirl,
In this verdant realm, watch the magic unfurl.
Amidst the grass and the clover so spry,
We dance with the fingers of earth and sky!

Boundless Hopes in the Foliage

In a garden where shadows play,
A squirrel wore a hat today.
He chased a leaf, so sly and spry,
While nearby birds began to fly.

The daisies giggled, wore their best,
In polka dots, they had a fest.
They twirled around with cheerful flair,
Each blossom danced without a care.

A bumblebee buzzed with delight,
Proposing dances in the light.
The roses rolled their eyes with sass,
As petals fluttered, full of class.

A frog with dreams of Broadway fame,
Sang loudly, never felt a shame.
While daisies cheered, and vines applauded,
The garden laughed; oh what a party!

Embracing a Verdant Fantasy

In dreams where greenery comes alive,
A tomato plant began to strive.
It fancied itself a giant tree,
Declaring, "Look, I'm wild and free!"

A ladybug with shades so bright,
Told all her friends it was a sight.
She strutted down the leafy lane,
Proclaiming, "I'll rule this terrain!"

The carrots wiggled in their beds,
Revealing all their leafy heads.
They giggled like a courtly crowd,
While joking, "We're way too proud!"

A sunflower tipped its hat in grace,
Knows well it's won this leafy space.
While clouds chuckled over head so high,
The garden danced beneath the sky!

Serene Melodies Among the Vines

Among the vines where creatures play,
A hedgehog strummed a tune today.
The melody was soft and sweet,
As butterflies began to greet.

The mint leaves whispered secret words,
To all the flowers and the birds.
They cracked a joke so sly and bold,
While laughing at the tales they told.

A chipmunk juggled acorns round,
While all the rabbits gathered 'round.
With cheeks all stuffed, they shared a laugh,
As nature joined in on the gaffe.

The foliage swayed in giggly cheer,
While crickets chirped for all to hear.
In harmony, the garden bloomed,
A comical world where laughter resumed!

The Garden of Unspoken Words

In gardens where the shadows dance,
A snail took part in quite a prance.
With tiny shoes, it made quite haste,
While gossip flew with every taste.

The weeds conspired, "Let's have a ball!"
As daisies blushed, growing tall.
Each stem predicted rain or shine,
With laughter ringing through the vine.

A playful breeze, a flutter here,
Had all the flowers lose their fear.
"Let's celebrate!" the petals sang,
As light and cheer around them rang.

A gopher grinned, that funny chap,
Then took a tumble with a flap.
In gardens filled with giggly joy,
Each plant, it seemed, was just a toy!

Entangled Paths of Enchantment

In a garden where giggles hide,
Rabbits dance, their ears so wide.
Plants whisper jokes in leafy tones,
While squirrels play on tiny thrones.

Laughter lurks in the rose's blush,
Bees buzz in a polka dot rush.
Gnome hats wobble as they prance,
Mossy shoes join the merry dance.

A feathery friend spills the tea,
While frogs leap like they're free as can be.
Dancing shadows on the sunny ground,
Tickles the toes that prance around.

With mushrooms dressed like tiny hats,
The butterflies sway, and the day chats.
In this realm of whimsy and cheer,
Every mishap brings giggles near.

Murmurs Beneath the Green Veil

Under leaves where secrets romp,
A turtle trips with a gentle plomp.
Chatting flowers knit their threads,
While the ants recite poems in their beds.

A sly fox wears a patchwork scarf,
Makes silly faces that make us laugh.
Caterpillars wiggle in perfect sync,
Falling off branches, they never think.

In this bright world of green delight,
Bumblebees buzz till they lose their flight.
Whispers float on a breeze divine,
Each giggle a secret, each smile a sign.

No frowns permitted midst the trees,
Only chuckles carried by the breeze.
Nature's humor wrapped in layers,
Giggles and glee from sunlit players.

Journeying Through Nature's Mantle

On a trail where laughter flows,
A clumsy deer trips on her toes.
A rainbow snail slides slyly near,
With jokes so bright that all can hear.

Mushrooms chuckle in grassy clumps,
While birds bob in their funky jumps.
The wind whispers tales of silly feats,
As ants march like they've won the streets.

In puddles wide, reflections dance,
Frogs leap high as if in trance.
Nature's stage, a funny show,
With plants that cheer and flowers that glow.

So wander free in this green maze,
Where laughter lingers and sunlight plays.
Every step a giggle, every glance a joke,
In this wondrous world, let laughter soak.

The Passion of Nature's Touch

With blossoms blushing red and bold,
Pollinators flirt, a tale retold.
Grasshoppers leap with a comic flair,
As ladybugs spin in the warm air.

The sun tickles leaves with golden rays,
While tiny frogs croak in chorus play.
Every rustle is a laugh in disguise,
As the wind fluffs up the clouds and sighs.

In this realm of playful cheer,
A wildflower giggles; it's quite near.
Twisting vines weave stories bright,
Inviting all to dance with delight.

So tiptoe through this vibrant mirth,
From the roots below to the sky's girth.
With every chuckle, let joy unfurl,
In nature's love, let the laughter swirl.

Wandering Through a Leafy Dreamscape

In a garden where the gnomes all play,
They dance in circles, but never sway.
With hats too big and shoes that squeak,
They giggle loud, their joy unique.

A butterfly lands on a sunflower bright,
Winks at a snail, what a funny sight!
The bees wear shades, buzzing to a beat,
As ants parade in a conga, oh so neat!

The wilting rose offers a cheeky grin,
While daisies gossip about the bumblebee kin.
Climbing vines whisper secrets of the night,
And giggles echo in moon's soft light.

So wander here, lose track of the hours,
In this leafy realm where laughter flowers.
Each twist and turn reveals a jest,
In a dreamscape where joy is the guest.

Shadows of Yesterday's Embrace

In a corner, a shadow plays hide and seek,
With yesterday's laughter, a blurry streak.
A hat of moss, perched upon a fern,
Whispers of secrets, just waiting to learn.

The sunbeams giggle, tickling the ground,
While memories spin in circles, all around.
Old shoes gather dust with stories to tell,
Of funny missteps and a squirrel's farewell.

The wispy clouds float, shapes taking flight,
A potato sack race, with a sprightly kite.
With shadows that strut like they own the street,
Each one a jester, a comical feat.

So close your eyes, and let them tease,
In yesterday's arms, let your worries freeze.
For shadows of laughter twirl in a chain,
In a world where the mundane is dressed up in rain.

The Lattice of Forgotten Whispers

There's a lattice of dreams hanging on a wall,
Where whispers of laughter caught in a brawl.
A hobbit with socks that don't quite match,
Charts the course for a fairy-tale patch.

The wind tells stories of fruitcake and pie,
While swallows debate about who can fly high.
A lonely toad croaks a raucous tune,
Challenging the stars to a dance 'neath the moon.

Old vines weave tales of the past gone by,
Of pranks played by squirrels, oh my, oh my!
They often forget and trip on their tails,
While scrolling through stories of mishaps and trails.

With every twist, a giggle takes flight,
In the lattice of whispers, day turns to night.
So listen close, and let laughter cascade,
In a world where fun is the grand charade.

Spirals of Silent Growth

There's a spiral staircase made of twirly vines,
Where the little green gnomes sip on sweet wines.
They toast to the stars with a clatter and cheer,
As the moon rolls its eyes, they hold back a sneer.

A cactus in the corner claims it can dance,
While the daisies laugh, "Give it a chance!"
With prickles and giggles, they move with a flair,
In a silent choreography, beyond compare.

The old oak tree snickers, its branches a sway,
"Life's just a dance in a funny ballet!"
The roots underground murmur riddles and puns,
As the bumblebees hum underneath the suns.

So twirl through this garden, let giggles take flight,
With spirals of joy that light up the night.
In a world where happiness grows like a flower,
Let laughter bloom in its mighty power.

Where Twisted Dreams Unfurl

In a garden where the giggles sway,
The flowers chat, come out to play.
Sneaky shadows in bright disguise,
Tickle your ribs with butterfly sighs.

Dandelions puff like fluffy clouds,
Whispering secrets to the crowds.
A worm with glasses on a tree,
Reads a book on how to make tea!

Bumblebees dance with a clumsy waltz,
While ants march in for the chocolate vaults.
The sun wears shades, oh so cool,
As laughter's the ultimate school.

Dreams twist and turn like pretzel knots,
Making mischief with silly thoughts.
Where reality bends and laughter swirls,
This is where all the whimsy unfurls.

Climbing into a Tranquil Reverie

In the hammock, the frogs read maps,
Planning shortcuts for sunny naps.
While squirrels juggle with lost acorns,
And sing loudly in weathered horns.

Clouds pass by on a slow parade,
Chasing shadows with a fun charade.
A sleepy snail in a top hat,
Sassily claims he's where it's at.

Butterflies learn to dance and spin,
Spinning tales where they begin.
With giggles that echo through winding trails,
Nature's lullabies tell the tales.

Sleepy sunbeams stretch and yawn,
As crickets play their favorite song.
This tranquil dream is a joyful climb,
Where silly antics flourish in time.

The Lullaby of Nature's Reach

Moonbeams plunge into cool streams,
Tickling fish in wiggly dreams.
Chirping crickets lend their tune,
While fireflies dance beneath the moon.

The trees exchange bark with a snicker,
As twinkling stars make the night flicker.
A cat in pajamas chases her tail,
Shooting stars wink; they never fail.

Freckles on the daisies bloom bright,
Saying, 'Join us for a moonlit flight!'
To twirl and swirl in a breeze so sweet,
Where nature and dreams delight to meet.

A lullaby drifts through leafy glades,
Wrapping whispers in leafy shades.
Underneath the starlit peach,
Life's funny tricks are within reach.

Curves of Green in Twilight's Glow

In the garden, a sneaky vine grows,
Tickling toes as the day slows.
Mischief stretches on emerald trails,
While chubby frogs wear tiny veils.

A raccoon holds a moonlit banquet,
Stealing snacks like a furry bandit.
The trees twist and laugh at their thrill,
Waving high their whimsical will.

By the pond, a newt does a jig,
While hedgehogs groove, each one a dig.
Even snails join the conga line,
Wobbling blissfully, feeling divine.

Nature's canvas, so vivid and bright,
Paints curves of green in fading light.
As twinkling giggles glow and flow,
In twilight's embrace, the whimsical show.

Ivy-Laden Daydreams

In the garden, I took a snooze,
Amongst the leaves, I found my muse.
A squirrel danced with my lunch to steal,
While I whispered secrets, oh what a deal!

The hedges giggled in a breeze so light,
As butterflies twirled, oh what a sight!
I chased a carrot, thought it was a race,
Only to trip over my own shoelace!

The sun decided to join the fun,
Tickling my nose, oh what a pun!
With ivy climbing on my dreams at night,
Everything starts to feel just right!

So here's to adventures, both bold and zany,
In a world where humor reigns, oh so grainy.
With every leaf, a giggle or two,
Life becomes a laugh, just for me and you!

Heartstrings in the Grove

In a grove where the laughter rings,
I found a tune that a loose vine sings.
A rabbit waltzed to the rhythm fine,
Twirling his whiskers, sipping on thyme!

The trees were jesters, with quips to share,
Waving their branches with so much flair.
A raccoon stood up to crack a joke,
While the owls hooted, giving smoke!

Hearts danced lightly on fluttering leaves,
As squirrels debated, wearing their sleeves.
The sun played peek-a-boo with the shade,
In this merry grove, no plans were laid.

So let your heartstrings pluck and sway,
In a world of whimsy, come what may!
For laughter's the melody we all should seek,
In the lush grove where humor's not weak!

The Language of Twisting Stems

Vines chattered softly in a twisted dance,
Teaching some frogs how to take a chance.
With every curl, a story was spun,
As beetles played cards just for fun!

The petals were gossiping, oh what a scene,
Whispering tales of the days in between.
A worm with a crown claimed he was the king,
While robins debated who would take wing!

Each leaf had a punchline, clever and bright,
Turning the garden into a delight.
Bumblebees giggled while sipping their tea,
In a world where chatter is ever so free!

So tune in to nature's comical song,
Where laughter and joy merrily throng.
You'll find hidden magic amongst all the green,
In the language of plants, a marvel unseen!

Beneath the Overarching Canopy

Beneath the big trees, where shadows play,
I stumbled upon a stray toucan's ballet.
With vibrant feathers, he danced all around,
While the squirrels cheered, hopping off the ground!

A parade of ants with tiny top hats,
Tiptoed along, in search of some bats.
They skated on leaves, what a silly sight,
Creating a ruckus, from morning till night!

The sun peeked through, like a spotlight's beam,
On this quirky show, a glorious dream.
The trees swayed gently, applauding the cheer,
In this forest theater, joy is so clear!

So let's linger beneath this leafy dome,
Where every creature finds a little home.
For in this carpet of laughter and lore,
Life's a funny tale worth exploring once more!

Spiral of Forgotten Thoughts

In a garden, lost in time,
There's a gnome that loves to rhyme.
He lost his hat and shoes, oh dear,
Now he's hiding from the beer.

Thoughts twist like vines on trees,
Bouncing 'round like summer bees.
A snail sings with a rusty tune,
Underneath a chuckling moon.

Riddles dance on a playful breeze,
While mice gather crumbs with ease.
What was that? A worm with flair?
Trying to be a debonair!

So here we sit, with our jokes,
Laughing at the wiggly folks.
All around, a merry mess,
In this world of silliness.

A Symphony in Twisty Greens

In the grove where shadows play,
Frogs have concerts every day.
They croak in keys that sound absurd,
As if they've never heard a word.

Breeze tickles every frond and leaf,
While squirrels spread gossip, oh so brief.
A crazy fox in a top hat sways,
Dancing through the leafy maze.

Mice tap dance on the clover beds,
Wearing tiny, fancy threads.
The chorus line is made of snails,
Gliding smoothly, leaving trails.

The ivy giggles, twirls around,
A comedy show above the ground.
Nature's orchestra, a lively crew,
Sings funny tunes 'neath skies so blue.

Where Dreams Climb and Flourish

Up the wall, the peas climb high,
Hoping one day to touch the sky.
Beans are plotting a grand escape,
While radishes dream of a cape.

Butterflies pull pranks on bees,
Spinning tales in the warmest breeze.
Each sprout believes it has a chance,
To win the year's best garden dance.

Sunflowers giggle, heads held tall,
Winking at the clouds, having a ball.
Their roots twist like stories untold,
In the soil, both stubborn and bold.

At night, dreams gather, plans unfold,
Whispering jokes that are pure gold.
In this patch of green delight,
Laughter grows, a true delight.

The Whimsy of Nature's Threads

Winds weave tales through leafy seams,
As the world dances on sunbeams.
A ladybug wears polka dots,
While ants pull carts tied with knots.

Caterpillars scheme for their flight,
Whispering how they'll be so bright.
A parade of blooms struts their stuff,
In fabrics of fluff, oh my, how tough!

The trees tell jokes to the passing breeze,
Making squirrels roll with ease.
Each petal flutters with laughter sweet,
As nature joins this whimsical beat.

We gather 'round, beneath the sky,
Sharing giggles, oh me, oh my!
For in this world of playful threads,
The joy of life never spreads dread.

Weaving Through the Leafy Labyrinth

In a jungle of green, I lost my way,
Tangled in tendrils, come what may.
A squirrel giggled, pointing at me,
"In here, you're not just lost, you're free!"

Vines tied my shoes; oh what a mess,
A playful vine gave me quite the stress.
"Can you dance?" it asked with a grin,
I laughed and tripped; where do I begin?

Beneath leafy hats, I met a chatty bee,
"Clamp me down, dance like leaves, can't you see?"
I stomped and twirled, made a grand show,
Until a branch grabbed my toe, oh no!

But when nature giggles, you must just join,
Each twist and turn brings a new coin.
With every leaf that tickled my spine,
I laughed with green friends—nature's design!

Flutter of the Green Heart

A butterfly whispered, "Want to play?"
I said, "Sure, but please, stay away!"
With wings of emerald, it danced in the sun,
Pretending to be a rockstar, oh what fun!

I wobbled and stumbled, right on cue,
A worm cheered me on—"You can do it too!"
We pranced and twisted in a silly song,
While leaves giggled softly, 'Come along!'

A ladybug drums on my shoulder so bold,
While grasshoppers danced with moves uncontrolled.
"What's the score?" I asked in delight,
"There's no score here; it's just pure light!"

Then clouds peeked down, full of glee,
"Keep this up, and we'll throw you a spree!"
With rain as confetti, we twirled in the air,
Laughing together—a garden affair!

Emblems of Nature's Embrace

A fern wore a crown of leafy green flair,
"I'm the queen here, with style to spare!"
I chuckled and bowed to my leafy friend,
"Your royal decree shall certainly blend!"

An acorn tried hard to paint itself gold,
"I'm a treasure!" it squeaked, but I was bold.
"You're a nut! You silly little seed!"
The trees roared with laughter; oh yes indeed!

A pine threw a party, all branches a-shake,
"Join us, whole forests, make no mistake!"
With maple syrup shots, we toasted with cheer,
While owls hooted loudly, 'The fun's right here!'

So here in the woods, let the giggles cascade,
Each leaf's a joke in this leafy parade.
Nature winks softly, all feelings embraced,
With humor and joy, we're perfectly placed!

Where Leaves Speak in Silence

Where whispers of green are heard on the breeze,
A leaf told a secret to giggling trees.
"Why did the branch cross the path so wide?"
To go where the flowers stretched out with pride!

A daisy chimed in, with petals aflutter,
"I've got the facts; oh, don't you shudder!"
But the wind rolled its eyes, taking a deep sigh,
"We're all just here to have a sweet pie!"

Tickles of sunlight danced on my face,
While shadows of laughter filled up the space.
"Join the brigade of the green and the spry!"
A clever old root raised its voice very high!

So let's twirl and spin in this garden of glee,
Where funny whispers are wild and free.
Nature can chuckle, and we can too,
Under these canopies, life feels brand new!

The Language of Wandering Roots

Roots chat in whispers, quite absurd,
They gossip about the things they've heard.
Pondering the shapes of clouds above,
They dream in shades of green, oh how they love.

Beneath the earth, they trip and fall,
In soil-soirees, they have a ball.
They dance with worms in swirls and twirls,
Laughing with the snails, oh what a whirl!

Each twist and turn, a secret code,
Forming friendships on the undergoad.
With branches laughing, they tell a tale,
Of mischief on the vine, they can't curtail.

So if you hear a rustle-down there,
Know roots are chuckling without a care.
In the land below, laughter takes wing,
As roots confer on the joys of spring!

When Vines Embrace the Twilight

As sunset beckons, vines get lined,
With glee, they stretch and intertwine.
They giggle and sigh with twinkling stars,
Sharing wild secrets from afar.

In dusk's soft glow, they start to sway,
Pretending they're dancers in a cabaret.
With leaves like tutus, they shimmy close,
Beneath the moon, they're quite morose.

They joke about shadows that go bump,
And spurt out giggles with every jump.
Twilight tales of critters and bugs,
Woven in laughter, like cozy hugs.

So when the night gives vines a chance,
They twirl and tease in a leafy dance.
In the embrace of dusk so light,
Vines craft their dreams in pure delight!

Cascading Hues of Memory

Memories flow like ribbons of green,
With whimsical shapes that dance unseen.
Each leaf a story, each curl a grin,
Reminding of times when the fun begins.

With dappled sunlight, they shimmer bright,
Dancing in colors, a tropical sight.
They poke fun at the passerby,
Whispering tales of that silly guy.

Each hue a wink from the past to see,
Like a pranking canvas, painted so free.
They flutter with laughter, tales to tell,
In a burst of colors, casting a spell.

So next time you notice hues that cling,
Know they're rejoicing in their merry fling.
The past cascades in shades sublime,
For memories are plant-fueled and full of rhyme!

The Veil of Botanical Whispers

Under a veil of leaves, they conspire,
Whispers of garden gossip inspire.
With every rustle, a chuckle flows,
As petals giggle, a tale bestows.

In secret blooms, they plot and plan,
Concealing silliness in their span.
The daisies tease the stately rose,
While cacti snicker from their prickly prose.

Veins of laughter thread the air,
Creating mischief everywhere.
The daisies twirl, the tulips bounce,
In a comedy of plants, they prance and flounce.

So when you see a garden bright,
Know the flora is playing with pure delight.
In the shade of blooms, secrets do wave,
Where botanical whimsies forever behave!

Lurking Echoes in the Ivy Labyrinth

In a maze of greens, I tiptoe so light,
Cautions abound, oh what a sight!
A squirrel's debate, one acorn to share,
With vines that tickle my legs and my hair.

A rabbit with glasses reads poetry loud,
While daisies giggle, joining the crowd.
Mismatched shoes dance on roots that entwine,
Each step I take leads to a punchline.

Behind leafy curtains, a cat takes a nap,
Dreaming of fish in a cozy mishap.
A snail plays the drums with a beat oh so slow,
In this leafy circus, I can't steal the show.

But laughter escapes from the heart of the maze,
As I lose my way in this leafy gaze.
Echoes of joy fly from branches up high,
In this ridiculous world, I'm happy to sigh.

Harmony of the Untamed Vines

Vines here are singing, a strange little choir,
With roots acting up, like they're stuck in the mire.
A frog in a tuxedo throws notes to the breeze,
While brambles compose with the knack of a tease.

Bumblebees buzz with a wild sense of dance,
Swinging left, then right, as if in a trance.
They caught a bold ladybug spinning around,
In this vine-covered stage, there's fun to be found.

Laughter erupts when the moon starts to glow,
As petals break out in a soft, silly show.
The stars, playfully winking, join in on the fun,
In a symphony that warms till the night is all done.

A tangle of voices, a riotous cheer,
In a garden where laughter and folly are dear.
We sway to the rhythm of leaves and of light,
In the harmony spun from the magic of night.

A Tangle of Whispers and Wishes

Whispers of vines play tricks on my ears,
They share all my secrets, and echo my fears.
A nudge from the ferns, a wink from the moss,
My worries dissolve, and I feel like a boss.

The wishes I make float on petals so bright,
A butterfly giggles; wrong colors tonight!
With each little flutter, my dreams start to twirl,
In this silly paradise, watch laughter unfurl.

Conversations of squirrels drown out all the noise,
While daisies debate if they're girls or they're boys.
A hedgehog joins in, offering his take,
In this tangled-up web that the garden can make.

So here's to the chaos with giggles galore,
Where magic's the norm and we always want more.
Each whisper is laughter, each wish full of cheer,
In this world of wonders, come join us right here.

Draped in the Embrace of Stems

Here I lay tangled, my limbs all askew,
Draped in this garden, it's a cozy zoo.
With leaves that jabber and petals that giggle,
Each stretch of the vine is a comical wiggle.

A tortoise in shorts tries to race through the brush,
While blooms hold their sides, in a hearty hush.
The sunlamp of laughter flickers down bright,
As the stems weave a tale that's a pure delight.

Jokes from the bark keep the laughter alive,
As roots tell the tales of their wild, crazy drive.
I tumble through flowers with glee and such flair,
In this bright, bustling jungle, there's joy everywhere!

So let the winds carry this whimsical cheer,
Down paths full of puns where the giggles appear.
In the embrace of the garden, I dance to my tune,
With each wild stem whispering, 'We'll see you real soon!'

The Allure of Climbing Reflections

In the garden, I saw a vine,
It twisted and turned, looking fine.
I asked it to climb, just for a show,
It sighed back at me, 'I move slow!'

With every twist and turn it made,
I wondered if it liked to parade.
It giggled and whispered, 'I'll climb with flair,
Just wait a bit, give me some air!'

A fence stood there, so proud and tall,
The vine looked up, and gave a call.
'Watch me weave just like a dance,
And soon I'll steal the spotlight chance!'

Now my garden looks quite alive,
With leafy laughter, my dreams arrive.
The vine's a comedian, I must confess,
Making climbing an art of humorous finesse.

Green Dreams Beneath the Sky

Beneath the sky, a leafy scheme,
The plants conspire, it seems a dream.
Their laughter rises with the breeze,
While trees shake heads, quite at ease.

Clovers giggle, daisies cheer,
'Come join the fun, there's nothing to fear!'
The grass below, it rolls with glee,
'Just plop yourself down and feel so free!'

But one brave sprout, with dreams so grand,
Said, 'I can climb! Just lend a hand!'
The others snickered, 'Come on, be real,
You're not a vine, you're a big potato meal!'

Yet with a wiggle and little feat,
The sprout surprised them, no defeat!
Now they all clamor, 'Hey, that's the way!
Let's grow together, and dance all day!'

Serenity of an Ivy-Clad Dawn

In the morning light, the ivy sprawls,
It clings to walls, and lightly brawls.
Whispers of dreams edged with dew,
Saying, 'Rise up, there's more to do!'

The birds chirp back, in playful tunes,
As ivy dances beneath the moons.
A vine nudges flowers, 'Join the spree!'
Together they giggle, all wild and free!

A squirrel looks on, quite bemused,
'Why do you all seem so enthused?'
The ivy grinned, 'We're simply spry,
In dreams of green, we'll never say die!'

So each dawn brings a leafy flair,
As ivy dreams float through the air.
With laughter echoing far and wide,
Nature's comedy is hard to hide!

Light and Shadows in the Leafy Maze

In a leafy maze, I lost my way,
But vines snickered, 'Let's come out to play!'
'Here's a twist, and there's a bend,
Just follow the giggles, it's not the end!'

The sun peeked in, casting light,
As shadows danced, a comical sight.
Branches waved, 'Oh, don't be shy,
Get tangled in laughter, let laughter fly!'

A beetle chuckled, strutting proud,
'In this green world, let's be loud!'
The flowers bloomed, with smiles so bright,
Their colors twinkling in pure delight.

So if you wander through this green dome,
Just know the vines are your fun-loving home.
With laughter echoing and shadows that sway,
Join in the jest; come play all day!

Beneath the Canopy of Stars

Under the stars, the frogs do croak,
Their jokes they tell with each little poke.
The owls all hoot, in time with the beat,
While fireflies dance on tiny, small feet.

A raccoon in shades steals a sip of my drink,
With a wink and a grin, he's smarter than we think.
He wears a top hat and a sparkly coat,
As he juggles the acorns, a true circus note.

The moonlight giggles, the night it seems bright,
As shadows of squirrels start a fun pillow fight.
The giggles are loud, though we do our best hush,
In this wild serenade, we simply can't rush.

So let's share a laugh under this cosmic sky,
With creatures so silly, oh my, oh my!
Together we cheer, under the dazzling glow,
As dreams come to life in the night's soft show.

Enchanted in the Thickets

In thickets so green where mischief must play,
A squirrel named Timmy leads all astray.
With nuts in his pocket, he runs with pure glee,
Shouting, "Watch out! It's a nutty decree!"

The hedgehogs roll by in a conga line dance,
In the grass, they're all twirling, oh what a chance!
A bunny in shades hops along with a cheer,
Saying, "Join the parade, if you dare come here!"

With a splash of fresh dew, the fairies appear,
They've wands made of twigs, oh, let's give a cheer!
With sparkles of laughter, they zip through the air,
Casting spells that make everyone aware.

So gather your friends, the night is still young,
In this thicket of fun, we'll never feel strung.
Where giggles abound and the stars give a wink,
Join in this jest, let your imagination sink!

A Climb Towards Illusion

On vines we ascend, what a wobbly climb,
With gales of laughter, we tickle the time.
A monkey in slippers swings high up above,
While everyone yells, "Oh, you must be in love!"

With bubbles that giggle, we float to the top,
Puffing out rainbows, we just can't stop.
A snail named Gary plays games of charades,
He's slow, but his puns? They'll blow your cool shades!

The clouds they all chuckle as they gently sway,
While giraffes on stilts declare, "Hooray!"
In this wondrous climb, we're dazzled and spun,
With each twist and turn, oh what silly fun!

Up here it's a giggle, with joy on display,
Floating on dreams that carry away.
Let's savor the ride and embrace the delight,
For magic is real, in the humor of night.

The Garden's Hidden Secrets

In the garden where wild things frolic and play,
A hedgehog in stilettos steals the display.
With flowers in bloom, they giggle and sway,
As they gossip about all the mischief of day.

The daisies wear glasses, the roses swift dance,
With whispers so sweet, they take every chance.
A toad on a throne gives the best of advice,
"Just smile through the chaos and sprinkle some spice!"

With veggies in chatter, the potatoes debate,
On who's the best dancer—oh, what a fate!
The carrots do cha-cha, while radishes lift,
The joy of this garden is truly a gift.

So let's weave through the petals, and seek out the jest,
In this whimsical realm, we truly are blessed.
With laughter as petals, let us gather and cheer,
In the garden's embrace, let's spread all the cheer!

The Pathway of Twisting Paths

In a garden of giggles, the plants conspire,
Raccoons throw a party, in hats made of briar.
Worms dance in circles, a worm tango delight,
While beetles beat drums till the fall of the night.

The bushes are gossiping, oh what a sight,
A squirrel steals a cookie, it takes quite a bite.
Tangled in laughter, the flowers all sway,
As bees break into song, buzzing all day.

Paths twist with mischief, where weeds love to play,
Each turn brings a chuckle, who's leading astray?
Sunlight pirouettes on petals so bright,
While shadows chase spoons that have taken to flight.

With every step forward, surprises abound,
A frog wearing glasses jumps up with a bound.
Nature's a jester, with tricks up her sleeves,
In the garden, where joy weaves a quilt from the leaves.

Embracing Nature's Soft Refrain

Bouncing through bushes, a frog finds a hat,
He struts like a model, it's quite where it's at.
A chorus of crickets, in concert tonight,
With fireflies flashing, it's a marvelous sight.

Dandelions giggle, they wish to be stars,
They twirl with the daisies, while swaying with cars.
Each blade of grass tells a joke with a twist,
The daisies roll their eyes, "Oh, take a big risk!"

The trees wink and chuckle, they bend with the breeze,
Offering acorns like snacks, "Would you care for a tease?"
The path is a parade, where whispers collide,
In this jolly garden, let laughter be wide.

Nature's a joker, in disguise with a grin,
Making merry, it loves to pull you right in.
With every sweet step, the fun grows and blooms,
In a world filled with hoots, and all sorts of zooms.

Whispers of Climbing Vines

Up the trellis, whispers of green beans abound,
They plot a new scheme, with a giggling sound.
Cucumbers gossip, they're all in a stew,
About carrots and onions, what shame they construe.

Vines tangle and giggle, they tickle the air,
With flowers that wink, saying, "Life is quite fair!"
Chasing the sunlight, they playful do tease,
While rabbits hop by, saying, "May I have cheese?"

A ladybug waltzes, on leaves made of lace,
She's calling all critters, "Come join me, let's race!"
The squash plants are laughing, a riot to see,
As they fight off the pests, declaring, "You're free!"

Among cheerful tendrils, a great laugh will ring,
Nature's hijinks become quite the wild fling.
When vines start their whispers, with giggles galore,
It's a garden of joy, who could ask for more?

Shadows on the Garden Path

Under the lanterns, shadows flit and twirl,
A cat in a scarf, with a whisker-like curl.
The moonbeams are dancing on roses and thyme,
As daisies recite their own nursery rhyme.

The wind plays the flute, serenading the night,
While snails with their shells, take a slippery flight.
A path lined with laughter, where whispers grow bold,
As crickets form choirs, their stories retold.

Singing soft praises, the tulips take bets,
On who'll win the race, the rabbits or pets.
The shadows are playful, they leap and they bound,
Proclaiming the garden, the best spot around.

With giggles galore, let the night be our guide,
Among jokes and silly pranks, there's nothing to hide.
As flowers all snicker at stories they weave,
In shadows, where dreams dare to laugh and believe.

Shadows Beneath the Canopy

In the woodlands, squirrels dance,
Chasing leaves like a wild romance.
Mice in suits twirl with flair,
Underneath the branches, in midair.

Frogs wear crowns made of old moss,
Jubilant tunes for the forest's gloss.
Every toe tap is a joke,
As the shy breeze joyfully pokes.

Dancing ferns giggle in the breeze,
Whispering secrets to the trees.
Laughter echoes in the shade,
A lighthearted, leafy parade.

Beneath the bows, shadows play,
Life's quirks on full display.
Nature's comedy, loud and clear,
A jester's heart, we want to cheer.

Embrace of the Hidden Climb

Ladders made of twisted vines,
Dare we scale these goofy lines?
Every step's a wobbly jest,
What's the rush? We're on a quest!

The squirrels cheer from nook to nook,
While chubby rabbits read a book.
A bear tries yoga, strikes a pose,
In rings of laughter, friendship grows.

Twists and turns, each bend a grin,
Lizards compete to see who'll win.
Nature's chaos, a comic spree,
On this wild, humorous tree.

So up we go, no rush at all,
Each branch a trampoline, we fall!
With giggles ringing all around,
Here's to joy that's easily found.

Woven in Nature's Spine

A tapestry of jumbled leaves,
Stitched with laughter that never leaves.
Breezy whispers, a playful tease,
Nature laughs like it's on a squeeze.

Squirrels play poker with acorn stacks,
Raccoons plot tirades for snacks.
Under twinkling stars in their prime,
The nights are silly, but oh, so fine!

Bouncing bugs in a belly flop,
Or a unicycle flower swap.
Nature's festival on this spine,
Brightest colors, endless shine!

So let's embrace this goofy art,
Where every twirl lights up the heart.
In the forest, joy does align,
With laughter woven, pure divine.

Dreams Entwined in Greenery

In dreamland where the weeds play tricks,
Gnomes make jokes about wild flicks.
A crow steals hats, so sly and spry,
Under the watchful, laughing sky.

Flowers yawn, stretch their petals wide,
While ladybugs serve joyride.
Each acorn has a tale to spin,
Of nutty worlds where fun begins!

Over hills, through the thickets roam,
With bunny guides, we find our home.
Worms tango, making rhythm divine,
In this garden, all hearts entwine.

So take a chance, leave woes behind,
Join these dreams, a twist unwind.
With every giggle, joy's the key,
In the greenery where we're all free.

www.ingramcontent.com/pod-product-compliance
Lightning Source LLC
Chambersburg PA
CBHW070318120526
44590CB00017B/2726